AF428254

HELLO COCO!
Suds, Songs, and Aunt Fancy's Salad

Latrice McGlothin

I wrote this book as a nod to the fun, magic, music
and food we create around our family meals.

My nephew Micah and my nieces Antoinette, D'Naya, Antoinae,
Chloe and Jade are a joy and can throw down in the kitchen.
It is my wish that every child (and child at heart) would be able
to explore the wonderful touch, smell and taste of yummy,
healthy food and that we would engage with them in the
journey.

-Love, Latrice

Hello Coco! Suds, Songs, and Aunt Fancy 's Salad
Copyright @ 2022 by Latrice McGlothin

For information address 2L Publishing, LLC, 5200 Clark Ave #548, Lakewood, CA 90714

Library of Congress Cataloging-in-Publication data is available
ISBN Hardcover: 979-8-9873170-0-6
ISBN Paperback: 979-8-9873170-1-3

Originally published in 2023 by 2L Publishing, LLC

For all the budding chefs, cooks, grillers and bakers
no matter how young or old you are!

Use this QR Code to
access and sing
along with the
Wash My Hands
Song

PiNK
COCO

Hi! My name is Coco. Today is a special day because Aunt Fancy is coming over. We're going to cook together. We always have a fun time because my auntie is a great cook. We make magical dishes!

Today's masterpiece will be a garden salad for family dinner. We have a big family. When we get together, there's lots of laughter, music, dancing, stories, and food, of course. It's fun to have everyone bring a dish. Aunt Fancy and I always make the salad.

"Hey, sweetheart," Auntie says. She gives me a hug. "Are you ready to make a yummy salad?"

"Yes, Auntie!" I answer.

"Remember... " Auntie says.

"Yes, I know, I know. I have to wash my hands."

Auntie winks. "That's right, sweetie."

We begin. Auntie clears off the counter. I grab my stool so I can reach the sink.

Aunt Fancy hums and does a little dance. I start dancing with her.

"What are you singing, Auntie?"

"It's a new song I made up to help us remember to wash our hands.
Do you want to learn it?"

"Yes," I say, clapping my hands.

Wash my hands; washing my hands
Wash my hands; washing my hands
Wash my hands; washing my hands
Wash, wash, wash, wash
Wash, wash, wash

"That's an easy song. Can we do it again?"

We sing together and do a funny dance.

Wash my hands; washing my hands
Wash my hands; washing my hands
Wash my hands; washing my hands
Wash, wash, wash, wash
Wash, wash, wash

Shine

When we finish washing our hands, I'm ready to take out what we need to make our salad.

"What kind of salad are we making today, Coco?" asks Auntie.

I run to the refrigerator and look inside.

"We have lettuce, tomatoes, green onions, cucumbers, lemons, olives, and red and yellow peppers."

"That all sounds amazing!" says Auntie. "Do you need help bringing those over here?"

"Nope, I can get it."

I pile the vegetables in my arms. Then, I head to the prep area and climb up on my stool.

Together we wash and dry the vegetables. Then, Aunt Fancy and I cut them up.

"See, I'm very careful to tuck my fingers in for safety," she says.

Our family loves music. Daddy is our DJ. He makes a playlist for every occasion. When the first song starts to play, Aunt Fancy and I take a dance break and sing along.

"Hey, what are you guys doing?" my big brother, Evan, asks.

Aunt Fancy smiles. "Hi, handsome nephew!"

Evan gives Auntie a hug. He asks her for some cucumber.
She tells him he needs to ask me because I am the chef.

I think about it. "W-e-e-l-l-l, I guess you can have a few pieces."

"Thanks," he says.

Just as he is reaching for the vegetables, Aunt Fancy clears her throat. She looks at me, then looks at the veggies and rubs her hands. I get the message.

"Hey, Evan. If you want some cucumbers, you need to wash your hands first."

"Oops!" he says. "I almost forgot."

"Washing your hands is important," I say. "You don't want to get yucky germs, do you?"

"No way," Evan yells, shaking his head.

"Auntie and I were just singing a song about washing hands."

"It's easy," says Aunt Fancy. "We'll teach you."

Wash my hands; washing my hands
Wash my hands; washing my hands
Wash my hands; washing my hands
Wash, wash, wash, wash
Wash, wash, wash

We dance and sing together.

Wash my hands; washing my hands
Wash my hands; washing my hands
Wash my hands; washing my hands
Wash, wash, wash, wash
Wash, wash, wash

Evan laughs as he washes his hands. He takes a few slices
of cucumber before joining Daddy in the living room.

"Great job, Coco," Aunt Fancy says. "I like how you explained why we need to wash our hands."

She takes a big, beautiful glass bowl from the cabinet and washes it out. After I dry the bowl, it's time for us to build our masterpiece.

"Do you know how many people are here, Coco?"

I jump off the stool and leave the kitchen. I count the number of people in the house. Uncle Jay, Evan, and Uncle Vince are already sitting at the table in the dining room.

Uncle Boo, Auntie Nessie, Granddad, Grandma, Mommy, and Daddy are in the living room. If I count Aunt Fancy and me, we have 11.

"Eleven!" I shout. "There are 11 of us."

Aunt Fancy looks at the bowl and nods her head. "This will be big enough."

"Okay, Coco, how do you want to build our salad?"

"First, I want to put in the lettuce, then the tomatoes and onions." I start placing each layer in the bowl. "Now I'll add peppers. Last are the olives."

Aunt Fancy laughs. She begins to toss the salad.

"Don't just toss it once, Auntie. Not one, not two, but three times!"

Aunt Fancy suggests we put lemon, olive oil, and cheese on separate plates so people can add their own final touches. Tada! Our mission is complete. The salad is ready.

"All right, I think we are good to go," Auntie says.

My family comes into the dining room, and everyone takes their seats. I place the salad bowl next to Grandma's famous fish.

"That looks great," says Daddy.

"I think this might be the best salad Coco and Aunt Fancy have ever made!" adds Mommy.

My smile is big. I am proud of the salad I made for my family.

The End

ABOUT THE AUTHOR
LATRICE MCGLOTHIN

Latrice McGlothin is the author of the "Hello Coco!" book series. A community and education advocate by day, an author, singer, and actress by night, Latrice received her Bachelor of Arts degree in theatre from Cal State University Long Beach. She loves to travel, play board games, her hubby, and beaches. Originally from Milwaukee, she currently resides in Los Angeles, where she most likely can be found singing her heart out. Visit her online at www.latricemcglothin.com.

ILLUSTRATIONS BY SOPHIE GARCIA
VISIT HER ONLINE AT WWW.SOPHIEGARCIA.CARBONMADE.COM.

www.ingramcontent.com/pod-product-compliance
Lightning Source LLC
Chambersburg PA
CBHW041940110726
48010CB00003B/161